PIANO · VOCAL · GUITAR

today's *Woman*
SONGBOOK

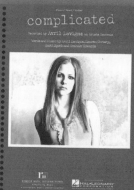

The Game of Love

soak up the sun

Cry

ISBN 0-634-06061-9

HAL·LEONARD®
CORPORATION

7777 W. BLUEMOUND RD. P.O. BOX 13819 MILWAUKEE, WI 53213

Visit Hal Leonard Online at
www.halleonard.com

CONTENTS

AIN'T IT FUNNY

Words and Music by CORY ROONEY
and JENNIFER LOPEZ

Moderate Hip Hop

Rapped: Yo, Mur-da Inc. Sung: It must

be the eyes. Rapped: They got me like, damn, if they get an-y fat-ter man the Rule gon' haf-ta get

at her. And our sit-u-a-tion won't mat-ter. I come to make you smile in the freak-i-est man-ners.

D.S. al Coda

I real-ly wish you would -n't send me gifts. _

CODA

- ny, _ fun- ny.
Ba - by, is that your girl - friend? I got my boy - friend. But may-be we can

Repeat and Fade

be friends, na, na, na, na, na, na. Ba - by, is that your girl - friend? _

Optional Ending

Additional Lyrics

Double D hi, double dose my fly by, red line, test the road side.
Oh I, never been a sucker for chump Ja.
Spit the ism hit 'em, get rid of 'em, and you know Tah.
Get it gully, and ain't that funny how they want me.
See me workin' wit money but Cali ain't a dummy.
What these brodies want from me?
'Cause all I got is G, J. Lo and Murda I.N.C.

BEAUTIFUL

Words and Music by
LINDA PERRY

Moderately slow

Whispered: Don't look at me.

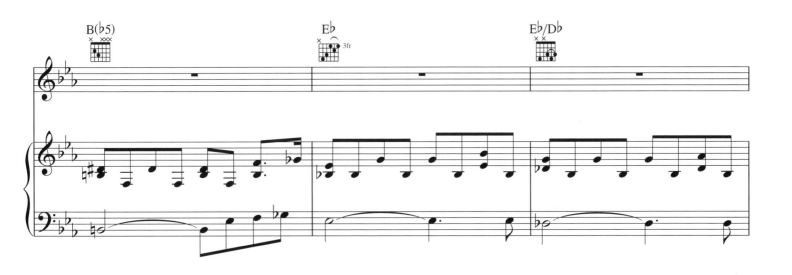

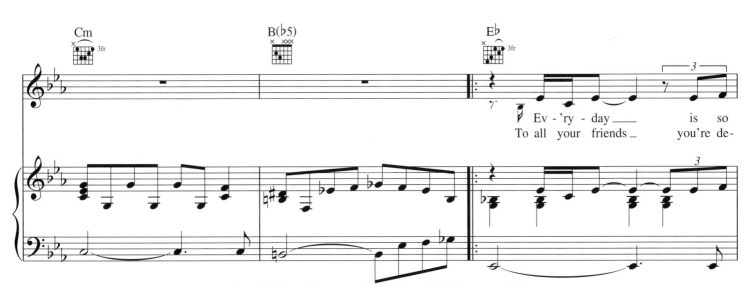

Ev-'ry-day _____ is so
To all your friends _____ you're de-

ANGEL

Words and Music by
SARAH McLACHLAN

Original key: D♭ major. This edition has been transposed down one half-step to be more playable.

BY YOUR SIDE

Words by SADE ADU
Music by SADE ADU,
STUART MATTHEWMAN, ANDREW HALE
and PAUL SPENCER DENMAN

Original key: B major. This edition has been transposed up one half-step to be more playable.

COMPLICATED

Words and Music by AVRIL LAVIGNE, LAUREN CHRISTY,
SCOTT SPOCK and GRAHAM EDWARDS

Moderate Pop

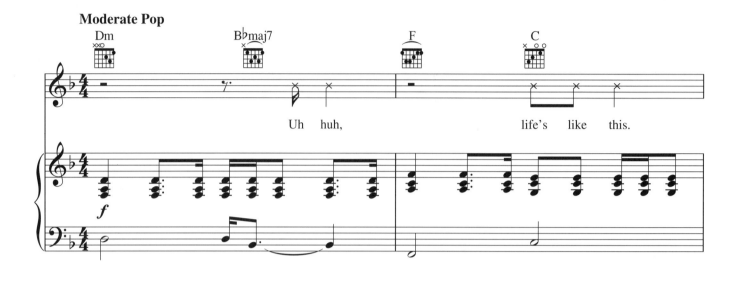

Uh huh,   life's like this.

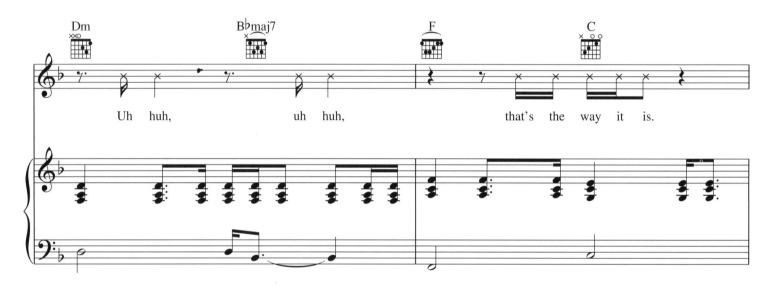

Uh huh,   uh huh,   that's the way it is.

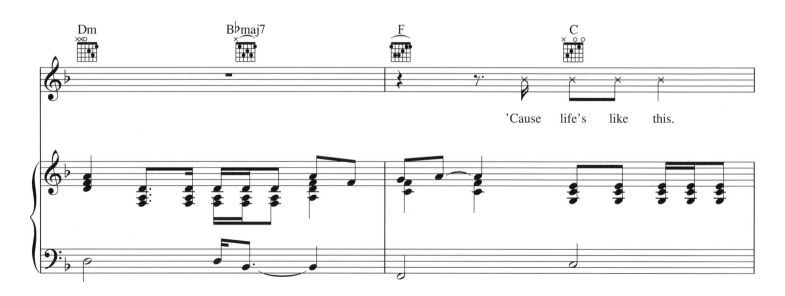

'Cause life's like this.

CRY

Words and Music by
ANGIE APARO

DON'T KNOW WHY

Words and Music by
JESSE HARRIS

EMOTION

Words and Music by BARRY GIBB
and ROBIN GIBB

Moderately slow, with a beat

It's o - ver and done, _ but the heart - ache lives on _ in - side, _
here at your side, _ I'm _ part of all the things you are, _

oh, _____
oh, _____

and who is the one you're cling - ing to
and you had a part of some - one else;

in - stead of me to - night? _____
you're gon - na find your shin - ing star.

And where are _ you

*Male vocal written at pitch.

FALLIN'

Words and Music by
ALICIA KEYS

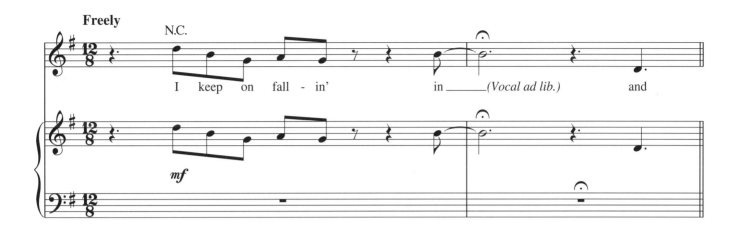

EVERYWHERE

Words and Music by JOHN SHANKS
and MICHELLE BRANCH

Moderate Pop Rock

Turn it in-side-out __ so I __ can see __

the part of you that's drift-in' o-ver me. __ And when I wake __ you're, __

Original key: D♭ major. This edition has been transposed down one half-step to be more playable.

FAMILY PORTRAIT

Words and Music by ALECIA MOORE
and SCOTT STORCH

GENIE IN A BOTTLE

Words and Music by STEVE KIPNER,
DAVID FRANK and PAM SHEYNE

FIELDS OF GOLD

Music and Lyrics by
STING

84

THE GAME OF LOVE

Words and Music by RICK NOWELS
and GREGG ALEXANDER

(Guitar Solo ad lib.)

(Make __ me feel good, yeah.)

I'M A SLAVE 4 U

Words and Music by PHARRELL WILLIAMS
and CHAD HUGO

Moderate Dance tempo

(Spoken:) I know I may be young.   but

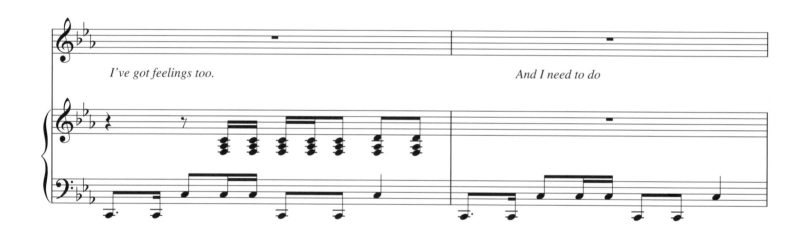

I've got feelings too.   And I need to do

what I feel like doing.   So let me go   and just listen.

I'M WITH YOU

Words and Music by AVRIL LAVIGNE, LAUREN CHRISTY,
SCOTT SPOCK and GRAHAM EDWARDS

JENNY FROM THE BLOCK

Words and Music by TROY OLIVER, ANDRE DEYO,
JENNIFER LOPEZ, JEAN CLAUDE OLIVIER,
SAMUEL BARNES, JOSE FERNANDO ARBEX MIRO,
LAWRENCE PARKER, SCOTT STERLING and M. OLIVER

Moderate Hip Hop

Chil - dren grow and wom - en pro - duc - ing. Men go work - ing, some go steal - ing.

Ev - 'ry - one's got to make ___ a liv - ing. L. O. X., yeah.

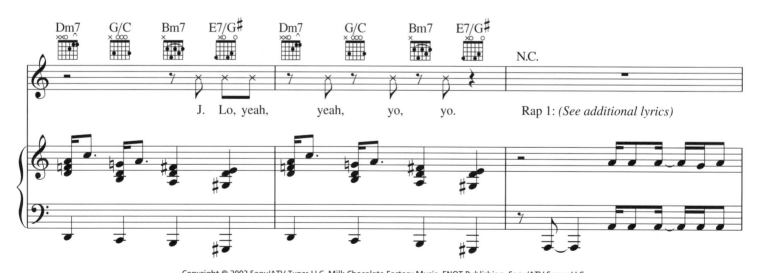

J. Lo, yeah, yeah, yo, yo. Rap 1: (See additional lyrics)

Additional Lyrics

Rap 1: We off the blocks this year.
Went from a 'lil to a lot this year.
Everybody mad at the rocks that I wear.
I know where I'm goin' and I know where I'm from.
You hear LOX in the air.
Yeah we at the airport out.
D-block from the block where everybody air forced out.
Wit' a new white tee you fresh. Nothin' phony wit' us.
Make the money, get the mansion, bring the homies wit' us.

Rap 2: Yo, it take hard work to cash checks
So don't be fooled by the rocks that I got, they're assets.
You get back what you put out.
Even if you take the good route, can't count the hood out.
After a while you'll know who to blend wit'.
Just keep it real wit' the ones you came in wit'.
Best thing to do is stay low, LOX and J. Lo.
They act like they don't, but they know.

LANDSLIDE

Words and Music by
STEVIE NICKS

121

UNDERNEATH YOUR CLOTHES

Words and Music by SHAKIRA
Music co-written by LESTER A. MENDEZ

A MOMENT LIKE THIS

Words and Music by JOHN REID
and JORGEN KJELL ELOFSSON

Moderately Slow

Original key: C♯ minor. This edition has been transposed up one half-step to be more playable.

A NEW DAY HAS COME

Words and Music by STEPHAN MOCCIO
and ALDO NOVA

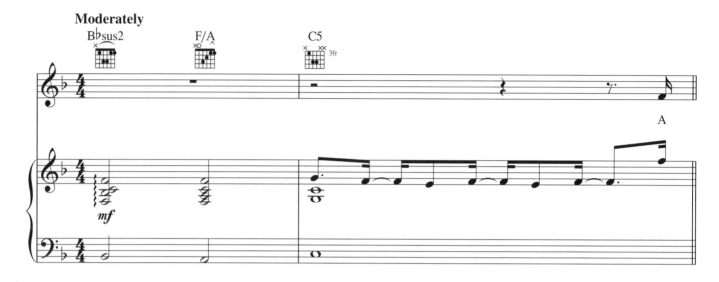

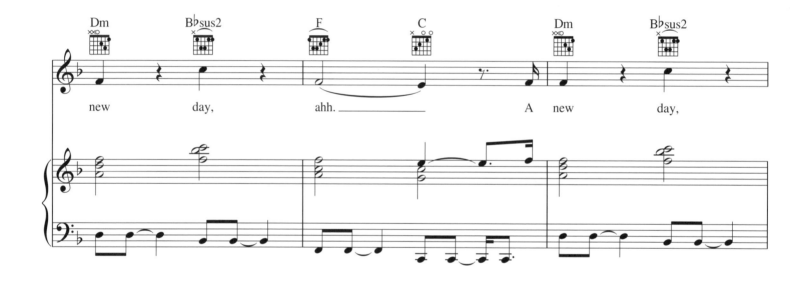

Original key: F♯ major. This edition has been transposed down one half-step to be more playable.

ONLY TIME

Words and Music by ENYA,
NICKY RYAN and ROMA RYAN

SOAK UP THE SUN

Words and Music by JEFF TROTT
and SHERYL CROW

SONGBIRD

Words and Music by
CHRISTINE McVIE

you, I love you, I love you like nev-er be-fore.

Guitar solo

THANK YOU

Words and Music by PAUL HERMAN
and DIDO ARMSTRONG

*Vocal written one octave higher than sung.

Original key: G# minor. This edition has been transposed up one half-step to be more playable.

Push the door;_ I'm home_ at ___ last,___ and I'm soak - ing through _ and through._

Contemporary Classics
Your favorite songs for piano, voice and guitar.

The Definitive Rock 'n' Roll Collection

A classic collection of the best songs from the early rock 'n' roll years – 1955-1966. 97 songs, including: Barbara Ann • Chantilly Lace • Dream Lover • Duke of Earl • Earth Angel • Great Balls of Fire • Louie, Louie • Rock Around the Clock • Ruby Baby • Runaway • (Seven Little Girls) Sitting in the Back Seat • Stay • Surfin' U.S.A. • Wild Thing • Woolly Bully • and more.

00490195 ....$29.95

The Big Book of Rock

78 of rock's biggest hits, including: Addicted to Love • American Pie • Born to Be Wild • Cold As Ice • Dust in the Wind • Free Bird • Goodbye Yellow Brick Road • Groovin' • Hey Jude • I Love Rock 'N' Roll • Lay Down Sally • Layla • Livin' on a Prayer • Louie Louie • Maggie May • Me and Bobby McGee • Monday, Monday • Owner of a Lonely Heart • Shout • Walk This Way • We Didn't Start the Fire • You Really Got Me • and more.

00311566...$19.95

Big Book of Movie Music

Features 73 classic songs from 72 movies: Beauty and the Beast • Change the World • Eye of the Tiger • I Finally Found Someone • The John Dunbar Theme • Somewhere in Time • Stayin' Alive • Take My Breath Away • Unchained Melody • The Way You Look Tonight • You've Got a Friend in Me • Zorro's Theme • more.

00311582 ....$19.95

The Best Rock Songs Ever

70 of the best rock songs from yesterday and today, including: All Day and All of the Night • All Shook Up • Blue Suede Shoes • Born to Be Wild • Boys Are Back in Town • Every Breath You Take • Faith • Free Bird • Hey Jude • I Still Haven't Found What I'm Looking For • Livin' on a Prayer • Lola • Louie Louie • Maggie May • Money • (She's) Some Kind of Wonderful • Takin' Care of Business • Walk This Way • We Didn't Start the Fire • We Got the Beat • Wild Thing • more!

00490424 ....$18.95

Contemporary Vocal Groups

This exciting new collection includes 35 huge hits by 18 of today's best vocal groups, including 98 Degrees, TLC, Destiny's Child, Savage Garden, Boyz II Men, Dixie Chicks, 'N Sync, and more! Songs include: Bills, Bills, Bills • Bug a Boo • Diggin' on You • The Hardest Thing • I'll Make Love to You • In the Still of the Nite (I'll Remember) • Ready to Run • Tearin' Up My Heart • Truly, Madly, Deeply • Waterfalls • Wide Open Spaces • and more.

00310605 ....$14.95

Motown Anthology

This songbook commemorates Motown's 40th Anniversary with 68 songs, background information on this famous record label, and lots of photos. Songs include: ABC • Baby Love • Ben • Dancing in the Street • Easy • For Once in My Life • My Girl • Shop Around • The Tracks of My Tears • War • What's Going On • You Can't Hurry Love • and many more.

00310367 ....$19.95

Best Contemporary Ballads

Includes 35 favorites: And So It Goes • Angel • Beautiful in My Eyes • Don't Know Much • Fields of Gold • Hero • I Will Remember You • Iris • My Heart Will Go On • Tears in Heaven • Valentine • You Were Meant for Me • You'll Be in My Heart • and more.

00310583 ....$16.95

Contemporary Hits

Contains 35 favorites by artists such as Sarah McLachlan, Whitney Houston, 'N Sync, Mariah Carey, Christina Aguilera, Celine Dion, and other top stars. Songs include: Adia • Building a Mystery • The Hardest Thing • I Believe in You and Me • I Drive Myself Crazy • I'll Be • Kiss Me • My Father's Eyes • Reflection • Smooth • Torn • and more!

00310589..$16.95

Jock Rock Hits

32 stadium-shaking favorites, including: Another One Bites the Dust • The Boys Are Back in Town • Freeze-Frame • Gonna Make You Sweat (Everybody Dance Now) • I Got You (I Feel Good) • Na Na Hey Hey Kiss Him Goodbye • Rock & Roll – Part II (The Hey Song) • Shout • Tequila • We Are the Champions • We Will Rock You • Whoomp! (There It Is) • Wild Thing • and more.

00310105...$14.95

Rock Ballads

31 sentimental favorites, including: All for Love • Bed of Roses • Dust in the Wind • Everybody Hurts • Right Here Waiting • Tears in Heaven • and more.

00311673...$14.95

0402